INSIGHTS INTO LIVING

The Sayings of Zen Master Nanrei Yokota

Edited by Engaku-ji

INTERBOOKS

INSIGHTS INTO LIVING
The Sayings of Zen Master Nanrei Yokota

Edited by Engaku-ji

This book was originally published by Engaku-ji in Japanese under the title *Irohanihoheto* (vols. 1–3).

First English edition: July 2016

Published and distributed by:
Interbooks Co., Ltd., Kudan Crest Bldg. 6F, 1-5-10, Kudan-kita, Chiyoda-ku, Tokyo 102-0073, Japan
E-mail: books@interbooks.co.jp
http://www.interbooks.co.jp/

Translated by Richard L. Gage
Photos by Ichido Uchida

[The poem on pages 3, 68 and 69]
English translation: Takahiko SAKAI
English consultation: Frances Ford

©2016 by Nanrei Yokota
ISBN978-4-924914-55-1

Printed in Japan

Contents

Preface .... *iv*

The Sayings of Zen Master Nanrei Yokota *1*

[Appendix A] Buddhism: Origin and Development *78*
[Appendix B] Zen and the Rinzai School *81*
[Appendix C] Engaku-ji: History and Appeal *84*
Glossary *86*

[For words marked with an asterisk, see "Glossary" on pp. 86–90.]

Preface

As the appeal of Japan becomes increasingly widely apparent in other countries, the number of overseas visitors to Kamakura, a distinctive ancient national capital, annually grows to the extent that, by now, non-Japanese visitors strolling the streets of the city are an everyday sight. As part of this trend, large numbers of foreign visitors are regularly seen in all parts of the Engaku-ji temple compound.

    They come for a variety of motivations and reasons. Some are merely passing by and drop in. Some visit because of recommendations from Japanese friends. Others are interested in traditional Japanese culture. And some want to experience the temple's beautiful, well-preserved natural setting. Assuredly some come because they want to encounter the Buddhism in which they have a prior interest or because they expect Buddhism to bring relief from the fatigues of hectic urban life. People everywhere and at all times seek answers to their doubts and confusions about daily living and the future in religion.

Keeping this in mind, I periodically hold sermon sessions for ordinary Japanese people. I say "sermon," but I actually mean simple talks, in my own words, on my day-to-day feelings and ideas expressed in easily understandable terms. There is nothing at all difficult about them. And nothing would make me happier than to learn that they became useful reference material for my audiences.

This book contains English-language translations of 23 of these so-called sermons selected because they will likely be interesting to a large number of people. Though the times and places where the peoples of the world live vary widely, I think that these talks will be of at least some slight reference and assistance to most people from other countries. Moreover I shall be supremely happy if they stimulate interest in Buddhism, Zen, and Engaku-ji, where I serve as Zen master.

For the numerous people who have no previous knowledge of Buddhism, Zen, or

Engaku-ji, at the end of the book, I have appended brief explanations of these topics and have included a glossary of specialist terms appearing in the text. I hope readers will use them as aids in making the reading material more interesting. I also hope that, from this small book, you will learn some new viewpoints and obtain some insights about living. Gassho.

Nanrei Yokota

The Sayings of Zen Master Nanrei Yokota

Connections and Encounters

Truly good people die while truly bad people go on living. Yet Buddhism teaches that the karmic law of good for good and bad for bad extends throughout the three realms of past, present, and future. That is to say, a cause always generates an effect.

We cannot know whether the effect will occur in the next generation or the generation after that; but, sooner or later, a good cause will always have a good effect and a bad cause a bad effect. But, since cause and effect are inextricably, inscrutably interwoven—through many different kinds of encounters—their relation is beyond our understanding. As this is the case, the effect—the thing that will actually rebound on you—must be accepted for what it is. It is impossible to alter a cause that occurred in the past. All we can do is gratefully accept what we are as good and sow favorable seeds for the future. Desiring to be what we aren't leads to delusions and suffering; realizing the blessing of being endowed with what we already have is enlightenment.

> Being born is amazing.
> Living is amazing,
> Let us join our hands in gratitude:
> For this supreme wonder.
>
> (Shinmin Sakamura, "Amazing")

When we consider the multitude of connections and encounters that result in our being alive in our present state, we cannot help bringing our hands together in reverent gratitude.

Cucumber Rejects

The other day, somebody asked what I think of the current environmental problem. The very mention of "the environmental problem" indicates thinking of the self and the outside world as separate. In Zen terms, it is a mistake even to speak of "the environment." Unless we accept the problem as our own, no amount of going on about the environment does any good. In other words, we must change our way of thinking and realize that the human heart has created the "environmental problem."

Today we tend to evaluate things exclusively in terms of they're being a little prettier and better shaped and whether we can enjoy them trouble-free, quickly, and conveniently. The current problem has arisen because we pursue such things exclusively.

The world of nature is dirty, unsightly, and ill-proportioned. Nature is as stinking as an old-fashioned outhouse. Recently people reject misshapen cucumbers as somehow flawed. In my mind, however, it is the cucumbers that are straight, glossy, and without insect damage that are "flawed." Misshapen, bug-eaten cucumbers are far more natural. I think we must revise the idea that anything other than the accepted shape is unacceptable. The self and the environment cannot be separated. Nature is all one.

Basically, when people quarrel and call each other names, the issue is always a clash of egos. Each party insists he is right and the other party wrong. Without this kind of ego-assertion there is no reason why fights should occur. But they do. Why is this?

Nature Nearest at Hand

What causes pain and trouble? The prominent cause is needless thinking (that we willfully create by ourselves). In other words, our own delusions cause us pain.

Zen Buddhism teaches us not to be obsessed with anything. The more we obsess, the farther we go astray. The more we worry about the nature of things, the further wrong we go.

It is better to forget. What should we forget? We should forget ourselves and, during meditation, even that we are meditating. Doing so unites us with mother nature.

Though we think of mother nature as something extremely elusive, actually our own bodies are mother nature as close at hand as it can be. Our breathing is the operation of mother nature at its most intimate. That's why, when we medi-

tate, we concentrate on and direct our attention to our breathing—especially to the spot in the lower abdomen called in Japanese the *tanden**.

The *tanden* and the abdomen don't indulge in useless ideas. People say that delusions interfere with meditation. What is the source of such delusions? The head. The task is to empty the head. Concentrating on the soles of our feet, as on the *tanden*, empties the head. A Zen riddle speaks of working things out with the sole of the foot. That makes sense because the sole of the foot engages in no superfluous thoughts.

Counting breaths too helps in this connection. At first, the act of counting occupies our entire attention. But ultimately, we forget the counting and even that we are breathing and enter the realm of unity with mother nature.

Impermanence

Generally when we think of impermanence or *mujo**, we have in mind the shifting, changing, and perishing of tangible things. From the standpoint of Shakyamuni Buddha's* enlightenment, however, impermanence means the coming into being and extinction of the mind, thought by thought and instant by instant.

The process of emergence and extinction is so fast that we don't perceive any change in location or circumstances. But the mind (or life) is like an old-fashioned fluorescent light. These lights turn on and off repeatedly but so minutely and fast that they seem to be on all the time.

Because life is emerging and perishing over and over again, it is never the same for a single instant. Because we are too insensitive to grasp this, we are deluded into thinking it constantly remains the same. We can, however, become

aware of the repeated emergence and extinction of life and its ceaseless alteration. When this happens, we realize that we, our bodies, and all we have are constantly changing and are therefore unsuitable objects for attachment. When we understand the meaning of the word *mujo* (impermanence), we realize it means the same thing as *muga** (selflessness), and *kuu** (infinite potential).

    We must accept the truth of impermanence as it is and live the life granted to us instant by instant and day by day.

Eliminating Self

Generally when we make plans for dealing with the various problems we encounter, we envisage things going the way we want them to go. This spells trouble. But, if we temporarily put ourselves out of the picture, we see phenomena as they really are and how they reflect on us.

Temporarily eliminating ourselves in this way means denying self-centered viewpoints, awareness, and judgments for a while. In Zen terminology this is called "killing the self."

Negating the self means seeing selflessly. This lets us see things as they really are. Thereafter, the wise thing to do is to live according to this view.

This kind of selflessness unites us with mother nature and enables us to appreciate mountain scenery, green forests, and singing birds. This in turn causes a boundless richness to fill our minds and leads to the cultivation of a compassionate heart, our ultimate goal.

It is important to realize that a very thin line separates what is in us from what is outside us. Zazen (seated meditation) is training for self-elimination. It enables us to "kill" ourselves and concentrate our entire bodies and spirits totally on what we are doing at the moment.

The Bottomless Bucket

In a certain Japanese folk tale, a rich man was unable to choose a successor to his fortune. So, he solicited some candidates and set a test to determine which of them would become his most devoted son-in-law and therefore worthiest to inherit his fortune. He instructed them to collect well-water in a bucket without a bottom. Almost everybody thought the task impossible and gave up at once. But one young man said, "All right, since my prospective father-in-law told me to, I'll do the best I can, no matter whether the bucket holds water or not." So he spent the whole night trying. And what do you think happened? Of course, the bucket without a bottom didn't slosh over with water the way a good one would have. But with each scoop the young man managed to collect a few drops in a separate container. And, as he steadily repeated the process, each drop added up until, before he knew it, he had a full container.

    This story embodies a good Zen metaphor. Instead of producing dramatic results, Zen training seems to produce no results at first, like drawing water in a bucket without a bottom. If you persist assiduously, however, little by little, something—like a mere few drops of water—remains. And before you know it, the accumulated remainder irrigates your whole mind.

Taming the Ox

Even after 10 or 20 years of practicing seated Zen meditation, delusions and interference from the outside world persist. They always will. Nonetheless, when delusions come, you can return to your fundamental self by standing straight, tensing your abdomen, and restoring your breathing. Shakyamuni Buddha instructs us to regulate our minds as a person trains an ox. When an ox wanders aside to graze on wayside grass, the oxherd pulls on the reins to force him back on the right path. Similarly, in seated Zen meditation, when the mind wanders, we call it back by directing awareness to our breathing as often as necessary.

In this way, we train ourselves to return to the basic state where we are always capable of calm judgments. Even then, delusion does not go away; but we can return to ourselves rapidly. Mastering this ability is called concentration or governing the mind (*sesshin**).

Guiding oxen and governing the mind actually mean the same kind of thing. Letting oxen roam wherever they want can lead to trouble. Keeping them under control, on the other hand, makes them a valuable work force usable to good advantage.

The unbridled human mind too, dragged here and there by desires, can lead to trouble. To prevent this, we must master methods and techniques of mind control. Our training aims to manifest our innate powers of maintaining our essential selves.

One of Ten Ox-herding Pictures*

Awareness

Vast, uncontrollable wildfires start with something small like a match or a cigarette. As long as they remain small, fires can be stamped out easily. But, left undetected, before we know it, they spread from tree to tree and finally engulf whole mountains in seas of flames. Then they are out of all control.

    In the same way, delusions begin with petty ideas. The more we think of them, the more such ideas congregate, causing delusions to get big on their own until, by the time we realize it, they are beyond control. For example, an initial minor annoyance, can grow into hatred, and finally into a homicidal rage. The situation is then irreparable. The first annoyance is only a single idea that can be eliminated easily. Getting rid of such ideas at this stage keeps people from going astray.

The connection of ideas causes us to deviate from the right path. Ideas will arise; there is nothing we can do about that. The important thing is to prevent their enduring by nipping them in the bud. Concentration on breathing enables us to do this.

Concentrating our consciousness completely on breathing makes us aware when thoughts arise. We say to ourselves, "A thought has arisen, I'm going astray!" At that very moment both the thought and the delusion vanish just as dreams end the moment we realize we are dreaming.

If we remain unaware of our straying, we can seriously go astray. The word Buddha* means one who is aware. Being enlightened means being aware. When we realize the triviality of our fantasies, we immediately return to our essential selves. Counting breaths one by one enables us to realize this and restore the self of the present moment.

Casting Everything Away

The India-born Jesuit priest Anthony de Mello* (1931–87) said that the person who has found a treasure for which he can abandon everything and no longer trouble himself even about death is truly living. The *Confucian Analects** say, "If a man in the morning hears the right way, he may die in the evening without regret." These words indicate that Confucius himself devoted his life to the pursuit of the Way.

How it is invested and the degree of our devotion to it determine the profundity of a human life. We ought not to speak lightly of risking our lives. But, if it is for the sake of the Way, we should all be willing to take that kind of risk.

Ability and inability are not the issue. The important thing is the resolve to devote ourselves fully to our duty, even at the risk of life. Such resolve has the

power to move great things.

    We should ask ourselves what we can do and what strength we can exert for the sake of the people around us. To do this, we must have the same kind of will-power that enables people to face a battle at the risk of their own lives.

Fish in the Sea

What if fish heard about the sea they live in and wanted to see it? The sea can be seen from the outside, but not from the inside.

No matter how they may want to, fish can't see the sea. And this causes them lots of trouble. They swim to the water's edge, leap above the surface, and dive to the seabed. While doing these things, at some point, they realize they are in the sea, that the sea is their location.

Zen training is like this. We are all the same as the Buddha nature. It's the same principle as being in the sea. We are right in the middle of the Buddha nature. Still we turn to outside things like other people and new books to find out what the Buddha nature is. But the more we seek it, the farther away it becomes. If you put your body in the right posture and observe your breathing, however, the

time will come when you realize that this is the Buddha nature. You will sense it with your body.

Fish too realize they are in the sea when they stop seeking to realize it. They understand that they were born in the sea, live in the sea, and ultimately die in the sea. We are born in the Buddha nature, live in the Buddha nature, and breathe our last in the Buddha nature.

We are always right in the midst of the Buddha nature.

Three Strengths

December 8 is Bodhi Day*, the day on which we celebrate Shakyamuni's enlightenment after six years of ascetic practices. Well, just what was Shakyamuni's wonderful enlightenment about? It was the truth that everybody, all living things, possesses the Buddha nature. And what does this mean?

In simple terms, it means first we have the strength to live and go on living. The strength to live tomorrow. Without exception, everyone has this strength from birth.

Second, it is the strength of endurance. I believe we can all endure everything that happens in this world. I also believe that nothing beyond our ability to endure happens. We all innately have the power to accept and endure the many different hardships and sufferings occurring during life.

Third is the strength to care for others. We are born with the power to pity and love, not just ourselves, but also the people and things around us. Seated Zen meditation is a way to manifest these three innate powers: to live, to endure, and to care.

Q & A Session with Overseas Students

In June 2014, fifteen lodging students from Yale University took part in a cosmopolitan *zazenkai* (seated meditation meeting) held for lay trainees at the Kojirin hall at Engaku-ji. Time was allotted in the meeting for a question-and-answer session in which students asked various questions and I responded. These are some of the questions they asked me.

Student : What is the goal of Zen?
Yokota : You are. The "you" sitting right there is the goal. After all kinds of hardship and suffering, you have finally realized that you've been here from the start.

Student : What's the relation between mother nature and Zen?

Yokota :   Zen itself is mother nature; mother nature is Zen. It's not a matter of endowing your body with some kind of special abilities. Living wholeheartedly as you are now is the Way. There's no other.

Student : Roshi, what does practicing Zen meditation mean to you?

Yokota :   It's part of my life. It's like getting up in the morning, washing my face, and eating. That's why I never forget it.

Student : How does a person know whether he has become enlightened?

Yokota :   The person himself knows best of all. Like you know best whether you've caught a cold.

Student : Why does Zen etiquette require us to eat soundlessly?

Yokota : First, so that the person eating can examine himself quietly. Second, so that noisy eating doesn't grieve hungry spirits who cannot eat. Eating silently is a way of respecting them. The idea is that we don't exist alone. There are other living beings that we can't see.

Student : What is the meaning of *mu*?
Yokota : The word *mu* also has the meaning of mother nature or "the grass grows." It indicates universal nature where flowers bloom and birds sing. On a hot day like today, the Zen riddle "Bring me *mu* (no thing)" might mean—among other meanings—"Bring me something cool to drink."

Student : How can we preserve traditions in the midst of modernization?
Yokota : It's possible to avoid modernization by, for instance, using fire wood to cook rice or heat a bath. On the other hand we can't live without things

like the telephone. Still, as long as we hang on to what is unchanging, we can conform to a changing world.

Student : How can we cope with temptations from the outside world?
Yokota : Putting on priest's robes makes us look different. And this is a natural restraint. In these robes, we can't eat at fast-foods eateries in town. During initial training, we encounter a few difficulties. But, we can cope naturally when we find new pleasures like reading books and studiousness.

Student : As a religious leader, don't you experience pressure from being an object of veneration who always has to give the right answer?
Yokota : I didn't make any special effort to get into the position I occupy now. Isn't it true that, generally speaking, pressure develops from trying too

hard or from hanging on to position and fame? I consider my position as one role in my training. That's why I don't experience much of the pressure you're talking about. That's the way it seems to me.

Student : What are the relations between Zen and other religions?

Yokota : I think it's possible to discover all kinds of mutual differences—scholarly and otherwise—among religions. On the other hand, we try to discover our mutual merits and common characteristics. On the basis of discovering our shared aspects, we can acknowledge our differences. In this way, we can avoid conflict and learn something good. We can discover the joy of learning from things that are different from us.

Working at 100%

Shakyamuni Buddha's mother is always represented in the upper portion of pictures of his death, or attainment of Nirvana (*nehan* in Japanese)*. It is said that Shakyamuni on his deathbed saw his mother and folded his hands in prayer to her and passed away. He must have felt strongly for his real mother, who died seven days after his birth. She sacrificed herself to give life to him, and he felt he should not waste it. Therefore, until his last moments, he devoted his utmost to doing good for others. He would have considered doing otherwise inexcusable. Finally, with his hands joined reverently, he must have thought, "Mother, I have done my best to the end. Have I done well?"

A certain Buddhist scholar has translated Nirvana freely as working at 100%. Shakyamuni died on one of his journeys to explain his teachings to others.

Throughout his life, with his whole being, he was always working at 100%.

We have all received an irreplaceable life from our parents and we must not waste it. Until the very last, we must straighten up and, at 100% for the good of others.

Brakes as Metaphor

Thinking too much lies behind many illnesses. Fretting can amount to self-destruction. Of course, thought is a good and important tool; but we mustn't overdo it.

In seated Zen meditation, when we think too much, it's time to halt for a moment. This is done by straightening your posture, locating your center of gravity in your abdomen below the navel, relaxing your shoulders, and breathing quietly.

Keep these two points in mind. Don't bother about what's passed. Nothing can be done about it now. So there's no need to think about it. In other words, if you go too far, it's all right. Thinking more about it won't do any good. Forget about what's going to happen next. It'll all work out. Then consider how wonderful it is to be living now, at this moment. When the seated-meditation session is

over and you return to work, think hard and long (otherwise, your work won't get done).

But you must always be strong enough to stop thinking when you are resting at home after work, jogging, or engaging in other activities.

An automobile needs brakes for sound worry-free driving. As long as the brakes are working, we can feel safe driving fast. In the same way, we need to develop techniques and methods for applying good brakes to our thinking.

What's passed is passed!
What will be will be!
Face up to the here and now!
Practice zazen and live while you can!

Zazen means meditating with this attitude in mind.

Leave the Rest to the Buddha

Leaving everything up to the Bodhisattva Avalokiteshvara (Kannon)* may seem weak. Actually though, it takes great strength. We can describe Kannon as the immense Buddha life filling the universe. It is the very Buddha nature in which we are all born, live, and die.

The Buddha nature is neither abstract nor hard to understand. Mother nature itself is another way of naming it. Mother nature gives us all a short life span. Having received life, we lived and die according to mother nature.

Sunlight, air, wind, earth, and plants and trees, families, and everyone else close to us are an only one part of mother nature. Right now, the important thing is to rethink our position modestly, realizing that we are sustained by mother nature.

Not knowing where we go after death is all right. The vital thing is to live fully and cheerfully as long as life lasts. If we can do that, we have no other responsibilities to worry about.

The Universe in a Grain of Dust

Recently the media has been saying that the discovery of what is called the Higgs boson* may explain the beginning and the end of the universe. We now know that the universe, which we used to think was mostly empty, is actually packed with elementary particles.

Science has arrived at the point where it can find a whole universe in a tiny grain of dust, like an elementary particle, and can proclaim that the whole cosmos is made up of such particles.

It has not yet, however, entered the realm of human consciousness, mind, and thought. Very long ago, Shakyamuni Buddha also described the universe as composed of dust and was enlightened to the presence of limitless universes in each and all grains of dust. This teaching is found in the Avatamsaka, or Kegon, Sutra*.

An old verse says, "Thankfully, there is not a single grain of dust lacking in the universal Buddha."

A certain nineteenth-century Zen priest taught that when sweeping, we must treat each grain of dust carefully. In its present state it may seem to be only dust, but it may actually have originated as part of a priestly robe.

In daily life, we must be respectful to each grain of rice and each cup of water. Thought by thought, in all things, we must be sincerely grateful. The Kegon Sutra teaches us to purify and adorn the world and the whole universe thought by thought.

The Sloth

We have dubbed these animals sloths, but I suspect they do not consider themselves lazy at all. In viewing the world, human beings, and society, as well as in studying the Buddhist realm, it is important to avoid adhering to any single set of criteria. Instead, we should adopt various viewpoints, value judgments, standards.

The criteria of the struggle for existence, the survival of the fittest, or natural selection do not explain the nature of the sloth. It is a marvelous creature that does nothing in particular. It sleeps for more than twenty hours a day. When awake, it eats two or three leaves from its tree and then just hangs there quietly in that same tree.

How does the sloth survive in the life-competitive jungle, where, in its absentminded inactivity, it might well be caught and eaten?

Many reasons are put forth to explain its survival. Its flesh is not tasty. Since it moves very little, there is practically no meat on it. But one truth holds. Things that do not fight or war are not attacked. Can it be that the sloth choses a way of life involving no fighting and warring?

We human beings pride ourselves on the civilizations and cultures we have created. On the basis of those values, we consider the sloth totally useless. But we ought to realize how small and narrow this criticism is when seen broadly and in the long view.

In the past, all kinds of creatures, like dinosaurs and mammoths, have appeared on Earth and gone extinct. This is in keeping with the law of impermanence. And, in keeping with the same law, the era of humanity too is going to end.

In the distant future, looking back on the history of the Earth, some creatures may debate what so-called humans did. If things continue as they are going now, I think the answer must be that they ceaselessly fought each other and grievously polluted the planet.

    Well then, what about the sloths? From the human viewpoint, they may seem merely slothful. But they live on this Earth without polluting it at all. In that case, perhaps the sloths are the truly splendid living creatures.

Keeping an Eye on Emptiness

In the morning when the sun comes up, though the empty space around us is illuminated it otherwise doesn't change at all. After sunset, the space around us is deprived of light and therefore is in darkness. But the difference is just a matter of appearance.

Something similar can be said about the human mind. When we are worried, in pain, or depressed, our minds seem to grow dark. But in fact, minds themselves never grow either dark or light. They may seem to darken because of all kinds of contributory causes. But just as empty space doesn't change, essentially our minds remain the same.

We tend to think of a Buddha as something pure, radiantly glowing, and free of obsessions. In contrast we imagine ourselves, ordinary sentient beings, as impure, foolish, and confused. This is what is meant by being attached to shapes and forms. Loud sounds don't break emptiness or space. A person can cause a ripple without being actually psychologically disturbed. Reasonably, things with form sooner or later cease existing. Emptiness and space, on the other hand, never change. That is why we must keep our eye on emptiness. It is the true mind of each of us.

Disinterested Frogs

All living things—Buddhas, human beings, animals, and plants—are one. In the summertime at Engaku-ji plenty of frogs croak. Perhaps my lecturing on old sayings at a temple may seem like an important thing. But there is no difference between my lecturing and the frogs' croaking in the ponds. Some of you may find the frogs noisy but, from their pond, the frogs never find the humans annoying or noisy. Still, they just go on croaking in their mindless way. And in that, they represent the real form of the Buddha.

How would you react to a frog that worried itself sick about doing the right thing or about the sound of its croaking? Instead of thinking too much about how singing prettier would help it become a Buddha, it just goes on croaking as hard as it can. Indeed, what else can be expected of it?

On the other hand, what might a frog think looking at us? Concerning someone who thinks zazen will make him a better person or wonders about the nature of enlightenment, a frog might say, "Aren't you already a fine person? Isn't it wonderful enough that you are engaged in zazen meditation? What else is to be expected of you?"

That's the way it is with most of our confusion and distress. Buddhas, ordinary sentient beings, and all living things possess the same mind. Instead of expressing all kinds of different emotions, that single mind is life itself. By life I do not mean the physical existence that at most lasts only a few decades. I am speaking of fundamental life. In short, the basic life that we all live is the same as the Buddhas, flowers, plants, and frogs. I hope all of you will live fully the life we all share equally.

Indra's Net

The Avatamsaka Sutra (Kegon Kyo) of Kegon Buddhism* contains mention of a great and beautiful net hanging over the palace of the Vedic god Indra*. Instead of being flat, the net is three dimensional like a jungle gym and has a beautiful jewel at each junction. Light from every jewel shines all over the net and reflects in all the other jewels to form a single jeweled radiance. All of the jewels are interconnected; none can be extracted from the net. The light from one jewel radiates throughout to be reflected in all the others. In short, the net illustrates the interpenetration of everything.

You and I and everything from plants to islands seem to exist separately. Actually, however, like the jewels on Indra's net, absolutely none are separate. Everything exists in mutual interdependence on everything, and nothing can be left out.

The lesson is that you and I and all other people live and are allowed to live in connection with the whole.

The Buddha who is related to the net as a whole and includes all the junctions is called Vairocana* (Birushanabutsu, or Dainichi Nyorai). The life of this great Buddha is the sun connecting all other lives.

A recent scientific view holds that the Earth and the universe are one life. This is in complete accord with the viewpoint expressed in Kegon (Huayan) Buddhism. The essence of the teaching of Indra's net in the Avatamsaka Sutra is that all things illuminate each other and reflect light in each other in the whole they inhabit.

A certain anecdote relates how the Buddhist priest Myoe* (1173–1232) once wrote a letter to an island. He is said to have brought his hands together in reverence and to have shed tears before some roadside flowers and to have bowed when crossing the path of a dog. As a practitioner of the teachings of Kegon Buddhism, he felt that nothing—flowers beside a road, a dog or cat sleeping nearby, or a remote island—was unconnected to him. He saw all lives as the same and equal and capable of sharing feelings. For Myoe, the idea of the sameness of all life was the natural way of things. His philosophy was that the Buddha abides in everything we see, including ourselves and distant islands.

Birds Must Fly

I consider prayer a declaration of being alive. Prayer originates in a declared determination to live intensely in spite of all suffering and hardship. Insisting on the need to live affects the mind of a praying person in a natural way.

Verses by the Japanese Buddhist poet Shinmin Sakamura (1909–2006) put it this way:

> Birds must fly;
>   we must live.
> Just like birds flying over the roaring rough seas,
>   we must live through the world
>   of chaos and confusion.

> Birds instincitively know
>> that they will reach the island of hope
>> after the breakthrough of darkness.
>
> Just as they do, we must know
>> that the future won't be a dark sealed book
>> but a glorious hope.
>
> On the morning of the first day in every New Year,
>> I receive the following proposition:
>> Birds must fly;
>> humans must live.
>
> (Shinmin Sakamura, "Birds Must Fly")

A little way ahead of us, there is no more darkness. For the person who constantly repeats "It's dark, it's dark!" darkness may go on and on. But for the person who believes in the light, brilliance is certain to break through. We must live. I express this imperative need in these words:

> Tomorrow is unknown,
> So live this whole day smiling.
> Our troubles may be many,
> So live this whole day with a bright heart.
> Unpleasantness may arise,
> So fill this whole day with kind words.

The spirit of the words we must live on is belief in tomorrow in spite of the impermanence of life. Surely we can all try to live this whole day smiling, even though tomorrow is unknown.

Napping on a Lotus Bloom

"On a lotus flower, happily napping a while." This is the sense of a haiku I once wrote, a haiku that would serve well as my farewell to the world. In the celebrated Chinese novel *The Journey West**, the monkey Sun Wukong* dashes frantically here and there as if covering a great deal of territory only to discover that, all the while, he has been running around on the palm of the Buddha's hand. In spite of all our many actions, we too, never leave the Buddha's hand, which in my verse I express as being on a lotus blossom.

The meaning of my poem is that human life consists of napping a while in the bosom of the Buddha's lotus. During the nap, we dream, sometimes sweet dreams, sometimes distressing ones. No matter which kind, however, they all take place in the palm of the Buddha's hand, or in the Buddha nature.

Human life is like dreams during a temporary nap in the great Buddha nature. While dreaming, a person can realize that he is dreaming and that it is all taking place on top of a lotus flower. This is the meaning I tried to convey.

Sogen Asahina (1891–1979), Engaku-ji head priest in the mid-twentieth century, strongly insisted on the importance of always believing ourselves to be in the Buddha nature (*busshin no shinjin**).

We try to find enlightenment* through zazen. We travel far and wide in search of happiness. But no matter how far we go, it eludes us. The important thing is suddenly realizing that our very walking itself is happiness. We meditate sitting with the idea that enlightenment will emerge at some point, when in fact zazen in itself is enlightenment. The issue is not entering a world of enlightenment where all suffering and sorrow drop away. The Buddha nature is right now, right here, in the midst of trouble and pain. The important thing is to believe this and proceed with a calm and expansive attitude.

The Ten-phrase Life-prolonging Kannon Sutra

The following is my free translation of the Ten-phrase Life-prolonging Kannon Sutra.

    My dearest Bodhisattva Avalokiteshvara (Kannon):
    Please save the people of this world from pain. The will to save people from suffering is the mind of the Buddha* and our mainstay.

This Buddha heart is the essential mind with which we are born. With the blessing of all kinds of connections, we can become aware of it. In this polluted world, the Buddha, the Buddha's teachings, and the companions with whom we study these teachings with point to a pure path where we can know constant caring in any situation, the joy of doing our best for others, and our true selves living compassionately.

I pray to Kannon in the morning and in the evening. With each prayer, no matter what I am doing, I act with a caring heart. In everything I do, I never deviate from the Kannon mind.

Appendix A

Buddhism: Origin and Development

Buddhism originated in India in the fifth century BCE. Together with Christianity and Islam, Buddhism is one of the world's three great religions. The historical Buddha, called Shakyamuni or the Sage of the Shakya clan, is said to have been born in 463 BCE as the son of King Shuddhodhana of the Shakya and his consort Maya and to have died in 383 BCE. Though his country was small, he grew up in a blessed and rich environment. Leading an affluent lifestyle, he became a cultivated, intelligent young man. At the age of 16, he married Princess Yashodara, by whom he was blessed with a son named Rahula.

One day, having departed the city by the eastern gate, he encountered an old man. Learning from this encounter that human beings grow old, he became deeply impressed with the fact that aging is inescapable. On another occasion, he went out through the southern gate and met an ailing person. This imbued him with the truth that human beings grow ill and that sickness is inescapable. Next, leaving by the eastern gate, he encountered a corpse and was astonished that human beings, who must ultimately and inevitably greet death, forget about death. Finally, leaving the city by the northern gate, he encountered a monk in training; and the sight of a person who had renounced the secular world for spiritual discipline impressed him so deeply that he decided to give up the worldly life himself.

When he was 29 years old, in the middle of one night, he departed from the palace, leaving his wife and child behind. He first trained under two hermit sages, one called Alara Kalama and the other Udaka Ramaputta. But, when he saw that this produced no satisfying results, he joined five other monks-in-training for physically challenging and punishing ascetic practices. At one point, he fasted to such emaciation that it was possible to feel his backbone by touching the skin of his belly and to touch the skin of his belly by poking his backbone. It is said that, in this state, when he tried to stand he fell over and that his hair fluttered down from his body. But he finally came to see that pointlessly punishing the body in this way fails to lead to enlightenment.

Realizing this, he bathed in a river and restored his vigor by accepting some milk gruel offered him by a village maiden named Sujata. Then, seating himself under a Bo tree, he resolved to engage in zazen meditation and not to rise until he had attained enlightenment.

And, on the eighth night of the twelfth month, while beholding the morning star, he was enlightened. The first words out of his mouth after this were, "Oh, how wonderful! All forms of life, all things, have the Buddha mind, which is able to see Truth!"

The three characteristics of Buddhist teachings are these: All things are impermanent and in a constant state of change. Nothing arises of this. And, true peace is the state in which the desire for worldly things has been extinguished. Shakyamuni went about, teaching his enlightenment, which finally spread abroad as Buddhism.

Born in India, Buddhism moved south to such parts of Southeast Asia as Sri Lanka and Vietnam.

Northward it traveled to China and Korea. From there, in the sixth century, it reached Japan mostly in the form known as Mahayana*, or Great Vehicle, Buddhism.

Mahayana teaches the importance of not concentrating solely on one's own enlightenment but on striving to guide and save as many people as possible. For a long time, faith in this kind of Buddhism was centered in Asia.

In more recent times, however, owing to the efforts of such zealous people as Daisetz Teitaro Suzuki* (1870–1966), who engaged in zazen at Engaku-ji, it has spread to the nations of America and Europe. At the time of writing, there are said to be many Buddhists and Buddha believers all over the world.

Appendix B
Zen and the Rinzai School

The Four Noble Truths and the Eightfold Righteous Path are called the fundamental teachings of Shakyamuni. The Four Noble Truths are: (1) Everything in the world is suffering; (2) Craving is the cause of suffering; (3) Suffering can be eliminated; and (4) the Eightfold Noble Path is the way to accomplish this elimination.

The Eightfold Noble Path consists in Right Views, Right Intentions, Right Speech, Right Deeds, Right Livelihood, Right Effort, Right Concentration, and Right Meditation. The Buddhist school called Zen (Chan in Chinese) emphasizes Right Meditation.

Zen, which may be translated as quiet contemplation, means viewing things with a calmly settled mind. As is witnessed by its being listed among the elements of the Eightfold Righteous Path, it is a fundamental Buddhist teaching. The first patriarch, Bodhidharma* (fifth or sixth century CE) transmitted Zen from India to distant China. Zen teachings were further clarified by the sixth patriarch after Bodhidharma, Huineng (Eno in Japanese; 638–713). As is illustrated by his neglect of meditative enlightenment and his stress on simple awakening, or *kensho*, Huineng put most importance on seeing the true nature of one's mind, which he taught to be the equivalent of Buddhahood.

Huineng's teachings were passed down from generation to generation till, during the Tang dynasty (618–907), Zen Master Mazu Daoyi (Baso Doitsu in Japanese; 709–88) further clarified the Zen teaching that the mind is in fact the Buddha. His disciple Zen Master Baizhang Huaihai (Hyakujo Ekai in Japanese; 720–814) established standards for training and living at Zen temples. Until his time, ancient Indian precepts like prohibition of agriculture and of taking life had prevailed. Baizhang Huaihai found his work of tilling the land himself to be a great help to his training. These teachings, handed down from Zen master Huangbo Xiyun (Obaku Kiun in Japanese; died 850) to Linji Yixuan (Rinzai Gigen in Japanese; died 866) evolved over time to become today's Rinzai School of Buddhism.

Though at first he specialized in study and research into written texts, or sutras, Rinzai ultimately tired of this pursuit as unsatisfactory and studied Zen as practical training under Zen Master Obaku. At the conclusion of stern discipline, he attained enlightenment and came to explain Zen with his own original expressions.

For example, he urged us to look to the true person in our shared bodies, the person that belongs to no rank. He said in a straightforward way that, if there were something the Buddha wanted to know, it was precisely the tale being heard then and there. A person who, seeing that the Buddha is the thing being heard at the present, stops seeking from without and becomes a completed person as-is, or a *buji*, person. He said emphatically that such a completed (*buji*) person is the noble—the noblest—individual.

Transmitted over generations, these teachings were handed down in the form of master-disciple catechisms. The Soto School of Zen, itself derived from the Zen of Bodhidharma, concentrates on what is called in Japanese *shikantaza* or single-minded seated meditation. In contrast to it, Rinzai Zen, in addition to zazen meditation, gives central importance to training in action and to Zen catechisms or koan.

In Japan, during the Kamakura period (1185–1333), beginning with the introduction of the Rinzai School from China by Eisai Zenji (1141–1215), one after another, priests from China came to Japan and built many Rinzai temples in Kyoto and Kamakura. But, in Kyoto, the capital of Japan at the time, older Buddhist sects other than Zen were so powerful that, initially, pure Zen training was conducted only in Kamakura temples like Kencho-ji* and Engaku-ji.

At that time, Kamakura was the capital of the shogunate, or military government, ruling the country. For the warrior class connected with the shogunate, Rinzai Zen became a spiritual support. It had many other cultural effects as well. For instance, the tea ceremony evolved as tea was introduced into Japan along with Zen. In addition, architecture, garden design, painting, calligraphy, and Chinese poetry flowered as aspects of Zen culture.

Appendix C
Engaku-ji: History and Appeal

Located southwest of Tokyo in Kamakura, tha national capital during the Kamakura period (1185–1333), the famous Buddhist temple Engaku-ji is the main temple of the Engaku-ji Branch of the Rinzai School of Buddhism (see Appendix B). It is ranked second after Kencho-ji among the Five Great Zen Temples of Kamakura*. A statue of Shaka Nyorai* (Tathagata Shakyamuni) untypically wearing a diadem and jeweled ornaments like those of a bodhisattva is revered as its primary image.

The temple was founded in 1282, in the late Kamakura period, by the monk Mugaku Sogen (1226–1286), who came to Japan from Song-dynasty China at the invitation of Hojo Tokimune (1251–1284), then regent of the Kamakura shogunal government. Tokimune, who became shogun at the age of 18 and studied under Mugaku Sogen, was deeply devoted to Zen Buddhism (see Appendix B). He founded Engaku-ji for the protection of the nation, for the spreading of Zen, and to mourn those martyred—allies and enemies alike—during the Mongolian invasions of the late thirteenth century. His teachings were handed down from generation to generation, and the temple became a central organization in Japanese Zen during the Muromachi period (1336–1573) and greatly influenced what are referred to as Gozan (Five Great Zen Temples) culture and Muromachi culture.

Over time, Engaku-ji came to enjoy the devoted support of members of the imperial court and of the shogunate, especially of the Hojo clan. Contributions of estates to the temple established its economic basis. By the late Kamakura period, the layout of the temple was completed. Time and time again, from the Muromachi to the Edo period (1603–1868), it was destroyed by fire and otherwise fell on hard times. But, by the middle of the nineteenth century, the compound, including the priests' hall and the Sanmon gate, was restored to become the foundation of the temple as it is today. After the Meiji era (1868–1912), numerous famous priests and cultural leaders gathered at Engaku-ji, which became the launching point for many significant figures. In addition, the temple is noted for the representative Japanese authors who studied Zen there, including Daisetz Teitaro Suzuki, who helped introduce Zen culture overseas.

The temple possesses two Designated National Treasures: the Shariden* reliquary hall and a temple bell. Numerous buildings in its beautiful grounds preserve the mood of the Japan of the good old days. People unfamiliar with Buddhism and Zen may unhesitatingly experience the free-of-charge zazen meditation sessions regularly held at the temple for general audiences. Men and women of all ages find the lovely natural setting with its flowers, wild birds, and autumnal foliage irresistibly attractive.

Glossary

Anthony de Mello (1931–87)
Indian Jesuit priest, psychotherapist, lecturer, and author of works on spirituality.

Avatamsaka Sutra (Flower-garland Sutra; Japanese: Kegon Kyo)
A highly influential sutra explaining cosmic interrelation; it is basic to the teachings of Kegon (Huanyan in Chinese) Buddhism.

Bodhi Day
Traditionally the eighth day of the twelfth month, December 8, Bodhi Day celebrates the day on which the Buddha attained enlightenment.

Bodhidharma
(fifth or sixth century CE)
The monk who is credited with having transmitted the teachings of Chan (Zen) Buddhism to China. He is considered the first Zen patriarch.

bodhisattva
In Mahayana Buddhism, a bodhisattva is a being that strives for enlightenment for the sake of all sentient beings.

Bodhisattva Avalokiteshvara
An embodiment of compassion, Avalokiteshvara (Kannon in Japanese) is one of the most widely revered bodhisattvas in Mahayana Buddhism.

Buddha
The title Buddha means "the enlightened one." In mainstream Buddhism, it usually, though not always, refers to the historic Buddha Siddhartha Gautama, or Shakyamuni.

busshin no shinjin
Having faith in the Buddha mind or nature permeating all things, sentient and insentient, and believing oneself to exist in that mind.

Confucian Analects
A collection of Confucius's sayings thought to have been compiled by his followers. It has been immensely influential in Eastern cultures.

Confucius (551–479 BCE)
The great Chinese sage and philosopher whose philosophical system known as Confucianism became a mainstay of Chinese and Asian culture.

Daisetz Teitaro Suzuki (1870–1966)
Japanese author whose works were influential in cultivating interest in Buddhism and Zen Buddhism in the West.

enlightenment
The English word used to translate several Buddhist terms but generally accepted to mean awakening to the true nature of things.

Five Great Zen Temples of Kamakura
A system of five temples organized to promote Zen Buddhism. A similar system of Five Great Zen Temples exists in Kyoto.

Higgs boson
An elementary particle named for the English physicist Peter Higgs.

Huayan Buddhism
→ *see* Kegon Buddhism

Indra
Hindu god or deva regarded by Buddhists as a guardian deity.

Kannon
→ *see* Bodhisattva Avalokiteshvara

Kannon Sutra
The 25th chapter of the Lotus Sutra devoted to the bodhisattva Avalokiteshvara (Kannon in Japanese).

Kegon Buddhism
Kegon Buddhism is the Japanese version of Chinese Huayan, or Flower-garland, Buddhism, based on teachings found in the Avatamsaka, or Kegon, Sutra.

Kegon Sutra (Kegon Kyo)
→ *see* Avatamsaka Sutra

Kencho-ji
A Rinzai temple ranked first among the Five Great Zen Temples of Kamakura. It was founded in 1253, or the fifth year of the Kencho reign period, hence the name.

kuu
The Japanese word used to render the Sanskrit term *shunyata*, often translated void but probably better defined as the infinite potential inherent in void.

Lotus Sutra (Sutra of the Lotus of the Wonderful Law)
One of the most popular Mahayana sutras, the Lotus Sutra (Saddhamapundarika Sutra) provides the foundation for several schools of Buddhism.

Mahayana Buddhism
A major branch of Buddhism, Mahayana—the Great Vehicle—is highly inclusive, insisting on the universal enlightenment and freedom from suffering of all sentient beings.

muga (selflessness)
The concept (*anatta*) that no persisting self of any kind whatsoever exists.

mujo (impermanence)
The concept (*anicca*) that all things are in a state of constant flux and change.

Myoe (1173–1232)
Japanese Buddhist monk and critic of Pure Land Buddhism who was famous for his lengthy journals.

nehan
→ *see* Nirvana

Nirvana
A Sanskrit term meaning extinguishing as in the extinguishing of a candle. In Buddhism it is widely used to express the state of serenity following the elimination of all desire and delusion.

Pure Land Buddhism
A branch of Buddhism widely popular throughout much of Asia centering on belief in the Buddha Amitabha (Amida in Japanese) and his Pure Land paradise.

sesshin
A period of intensive zazen meditation.

Shaka Nyorai (Tathagata Shakyamuni)
An epithet applied to Shakyamuni, the historical Buddha, meaning something like the Enlightened Sage of the Shakya clan.

Shakyamuni
→ *see* Shakyamuni Buddha

Shakyamuni Buddha
Shakyamuni (the sage of the Shakya clan) is a term often applied to Siddhartha Gautama, the historical Buddha.

shariden
Shariden is a Japanese word meaning reliquary hall. One of the most celebrated in Japan is the Shariden at Engaku-ji.

Shinmin Sakamura (1909–2006)
Japanese Buddhist poet.

Sun Wukong
Also known as the Monkey King, Sun Wukong (Son Goku in Japanese) is a leading character in the Chinese novel *The Journey West* (*Journey to the West*).

tanden (Chinese: *dantian*)
A spot below the navel which Buddhist teachings consider a useful object of concentration for controlling thought and emotions during meditation.

Tendai Buddhism
Tendai is a Japanese school of Buddhism based on the teachings of the Lotus Sutra and descended from Chinese Tiantai Buddhism.

Ten Ox-herding Pictures
A series of poems and pictures used in Zen Buddhism to illustrate stages of progress toward enlightenment and mental purification.

The Journey West (*Journey to the West*)
A great sixteenth-century Chinese novel dealing with legendary adventures loosely connected with the pilgrimage of the monk Xuanzang, who traveled "West"—that is to Central Asia and India—in search of sacred Buddhist texts.

The Ten-phrase Life-prolonging Kannon Sutra (Japanese: Enmei Jikku Kannon Kyo)
A devotional chant to the Bodhisattva Avalokiteshvara (Kannon), said to be based on the Kannon Sutra, the 25th chapter of the Lotus Sutra.

Vairocana (Japanese: Birushanabutsu or Dainichi Nyorai)
A primordial Buddha important in Japanese Kegon and Tendai Buddhism.

Xuanzang (602–64)
Chinese monk, scholar, and translator famous for his travels throughout Asia in search of Buddhist scriptures. The main character in the Chinese novel *The Journey West* is based on Xuanzang.